A Countryman's Year

MARKET DAY, TENTERDEN
by Fred Roe RI

A COUNTRYMAN'S YEAR

reflections of a village parson

'OLIVER'

by John Green

SALMON

Published by
J. Salmon Limited
100 London Road, Sevenoaks, Kent TN13 1BB

First Edition 1994

Designed by the Salmon Studio

Text copyright © John Green
Illustrations copyright ©1994 J. Salmon Limited

Limpbound ISBN 1 898435 19 7
Hardback ISBN 1 898435 20 0

Printed in England by
J. Salmon Limited
Tubs Hill Works
Sevenoaks

FOREWORD

I suppose that my love of the countryside all began in a Kent cherry orchard. My father's spacious rectory was surrounded on three sides by cherry orchards and beyond them were acres of hop gardens. My daily walks became a joy and an education. Small boys are naturally inquisitive, so questions flowed and knowledge unconsciously grew. Specially exciting was cherry-picking time; cherries seemed to shower down onto the ground and we daily returned home with a basket overflowing. Then came hop-picking in September, with the invasion of East Enders from London and its own special camaraderie in the hop gardens. Finally, but not least, there was the smell, all-pervading, in the oasts and seeming to penetrate both clothing and hair. Many is the time that I stood, wide-eyed, at the kiln watching the men at work and longing to be one of them. Even now, each new season, that smell – exciting, intoxicating – causes my heart to miss a beat and I am momentarily back in my childhood. Later, my father moved across the county and his new country parish embraced a large heronry and some of Romney Marsh. New discoveries, new bird life and the romantic 'atmosphere' of the Marsh and unknowingly I was captivated and fell in love with that Fifth Quarter of the Globe.

Then in the background were my two uncles – one a botanist (but, sadly, resident in London) and the other a well-known entomologist, his large study full of boxes and apparatus and cabinets. Open them and you might see a privet hawk moth caterpillar or rows of fritillaries. It was not long before he enthused me and gave me a sound and sensitive understanding of that fascinating and gentle world of moth and butterfly. Years later I had the privilege of my own country parishes in Kent. Large rectory gardens were surrounded by the whole range of countryside – open marshland, downland (with orchids), cherry orchards and hop gardens and the undulating Wealden farmland. Regularly involved in writing sermons and letters and articles for my parish magazine, I soon felt impelled to write about the countryside as well and to open people's eyes to the wonders around them daily. So "A Countryman's Notebook" was born and introduced into the magazine and the local paper.

I long to be a tiny cog in the ever-growing movement to understand and care for our countryside and its wildlife, under constant threat from the demands of our modern, technological society. This threat is particularly strong at present in my beloved Kent, once fondly named the Garden of England. I also long to help people tune in to the balance and slow rhythm of the countryside so that, in the end, every walk is full of interest, every day seems a holiday and in every direction they can see God.

Rolvenden, Kent 1994   John Green

JANUARY

JANUARY can be a 'hard' month in the country-side – no growth, no colour, and little wildlife movement. And yet this is only partly true, ever. For instance, there is a 200 yard hedge in the fields behind the rectory, uncut for three years, and it is full of colour to sensitive eyes. Last week early morning sunshine brought out its variety and colouring even more obviously. Outstanding were the vermilion hips of clumps of dog rose, but these were against a backcloth of many other quieter colours – areas of privet, still with its dark green leaves and black berries; small hedgerow oaks, a few leaves still clinging and failing to hide brown oak apples; two self-sown sycamore, still retaining many brown papery 'wings', and, here and there, numerous very wizened blackberries and some stumpy hazel catkins, the one a survivor and the other a forerunner, a herald of things to come – suggestive of primroses and long yellowy catkins shedding their pollen in a spring breeze.

And now – the snow. Two days of intermittent heavy falls and sub-zero temperatures. It is another world, in this open countryside. The hedge is virtually hidden, but is still a resting point for fieldfares, titmice and linnets and, in its roots, a warm shelter with limited food for small mammals and wrens. As I walked Oliver, our Jack Russell, at breakfast time, the only tracks on our path were of a fox who had clearly turned off into the rectory copse, gone along the paddock boundary and down to the pond in search of an unwary mallard. This morning eight mallard were crowded onto the only unfrozen piece of water (scarcely 3ft x 3ft) in-variably different from the remainder and caused by a slight but steady inflow from the road. Two moorhens flew up off the ice, landing about 200 feet up in a tree, always a little unexpected but reminding me that they do occasionally nest up a tree instead of in reeds or bushes near the water. Another sign of extreme weather drawing birds closer was when a snipe flew out of a hedge nearby and zigzagged off towards Old Place and the marsh.

Finally, of course, the bird-table is the scene of great activity. Special pleasure came when a greater spotted woodpecker twice patronised it. Happily also there is a very large skimmia bush close by. This is specially valuable in this extreme weather; inside is sufficient shelter for about 50–60 birds and round its roots leaf humus of many years standing which must continue to yield natural food in spite of snow and ice.

WALKING along the banks of the Rother at Newenden is a special experience – quite different

WINTER – SNARGATE, ROMNEY MARSH
by John Doyle RWS

from the track round Sandhurst's Old Place Farm or the footpath to Bourne Farm. There is for me the feel of Romney Marsh (after all, the Rother once joined the sea at New Romney), wide open skies, a certain loneliness and always the changing mood of the river. The other day it was semi-frozen and 26 mute swans glided up-river like some fleet of graceful ice-breakers. Comparing cygnets and adults it seemed as if three family parties had joined forces, driven together by the frozen state of many dykes in the valley. Over to my left one of the local kestrels was standing sentinel on a post at the sewage farm, where sooner or later a rat was bound to appear. Nearer to us, several black-headed gulls were standing on the furrows, fat and undecided, wondering where to scavenge next. On the bank itself the only stirring was from a few skylarks and a robin and a thrush, these last two looking forlorn and out of place. Suddenly Oliver pounced, muzzle driven into the ground – a mole run, clearly! Great excitement and digging, but no luck. A fisherman homeward bound exchanged a greeting from the other bank, oblivious of his shadow in the water, superbly clear in the light of the waning winter sun. In the end Oliver and I turned for home. By this time the mist was lying low over Selmes' Meadows, camouflaging the dog and sharpening the usual scents of dusk. An experience indeed. Robert Gibbings ought to have written a book entitled "Coming down the Rother" as a companion to his delightful volume on the Thames.

THERE are few things more graceful than the curved neck of a mute swan or more exciting than the loud singing note of its wing-beat. So I am delighted that swans are the subject of the first pictorial stamps of the new year. After all, they bear the *cachet* of royalty and they are majestic indeed in flight. Near me, on the Rother Levels, they foregather in the winter, on the stretch between Smallhythe and Rolvenden when the weather worsens on Romney Marsh itself. Last year one particular field carried about a hundred mute swans for weeks; this year a smaller flock have been wintering on another neighbouring field and presumably roosting at night on the dykes and channels closeby. As I write, Potman's Heath Channel is flooded as far as Maytham Wharf – a choice of acres of water. The smaller Bewick's swan is also present in fair numbers on Romney Marsh this month, particularly on the gravel pits near Lydd. Swans also bring back memories of power failures. In the 1960s it was an accepted hazard of living in the Marsh. Sadly, a swan flew into a power line about once a month, so candles and pressure lamps were kept at the ready and often used. Happily such tragedies happen less frequently these days.

Mention of candles allows me to introduce

church mice, beloved by John Betjeman. J.B.'s mouse was a resident and allegedly religious and resented outsiders invading his preserves at Harvest Festival, when there was richer fare than old service-books, half-split hassocks and burnt-down altar candles. Post-Christmas a mouse whizzed around between vestry and baptistry in Rolvenden church all one Sunday. Even bolder was the mouse observed today in the great parish church of All Saints, Maidstone. In the presence of choir, orchestra and a large congregation made up of the High Sheriff, Her Majesty's Judges, barristers and magistrates, it wriggled up the many steps into the north aisle in search of that hidden floor polish or store of oasis or perhaps just a little peace and quiet. It is also highly risky to mention church mice to organ builders and tuners. Their pulses race. Mice have been known to build nests in organ cases, eat leather work in their innards and even, believe it or not, chew through lead pipes. Specially, though, do I remember a *cri de coeur* written in the tuner's book on the little organ in Bonnington church beside the Royal Military Canal. "Get rid of those mice before next time or else . . ."

Assumptions can be dangerous and humbling. No sooner had I written that swans seldom fly into the power lines these days than I came across exactly that, half a mile away. There remained at my feet only a small cluster of soft, white downy feathers, all that was left of two mute swans which had been blown onto the lines near Potman's Heath by those gale force winds of January 13th. Nature, personified perhaps by a fox or two, had quietly cleared away the remains of those two majestic birds.

LAST week on Saturday and Sunday evenings Oliver's eyes were drawn to the TV screen and stayed there. He could hardly believe his eyes. Things on four legs (in one case, even these were not visible) were parading in front of the judges at Cruft's. He almost wrote the letter that appeared in Monday's *Daily Telegraph*, drafted by another Jack Russell and his master from Cambridge, expressing amazement at the lengths some dog-owners go to produce show specimens. He is very concerned for his cousin JRs who do reach Cruft's and hopes that their natural independence and toughness will sustain them against the might of breeding methods. We were both relieved that two well-known and recognisable dogs – an Irish Setter and an Irish Wolfhound – were champion and runner-up respectively. We also gave top marks to the Essex Dog Display team who specialise in rehabilitating ill-treated, unwanted dogs. We were treated to a delightful exhibition of various breeds and mongrels happily showing their paces on a doggy obstacle course. One mongrel had been thrown out of a car

AN ENGLISH LANE
by J. C. T. Willis

at 60 mph; it almost beggars belief!

So another Cruft's has come to an end. At least one leading canine magazine did not send a representative – "it is losing its atmosphere and allowing extremes to prevail". Oliver considers that he is well out of it. In spite of the eulogies of the TV commentators who seem to label most entrants as "tremendous hunters", he wonders if some could even run. So he boosted his ego the next morning with a good chase.

PAPERWORK in the study was proving unusually oppressive, so I took one of the best antidotes – a slow stroll round the garden. No matter that it was mid-winter and a dull, cloudy day; there would be something to see and to cheer. Sure enough, in front of the tool-shed, contending with layers of wet leaves and occasional pony hooves, were numerous daffodil spikes. Round the corner, partially covered by more beech leaves, was our Christmas rose, in its second year, promising several flowers very soon; a pale delicate offering for the flower-arranger. Almost overhanging it were clusters of hazel catkins, another hopeful sign; they had been there in an undeveloped state since the autumn when the grey squirrels were ravaging the few nuts there were; now they were gradually loosening, until by February they would be long and pliant and yellow with pollen. Of course, there were other hopeful signs – tight buds on the deep-red camellia, sticky horse-chestnut buds (which I can never resist touching!) and similar signs on a nearby sycamore, with some of last year's scimitar-shaped seeds still clinging. Here and there, too, were flowers. Three blooms still held on the 'Iceberg' rose in the border, heathers lent a touch of pinky mauve, a winter-flowering cherry was just showing red and our jasmine offered a great spread of yellow to all our visitors. We could not boast, as could one parishioner, of snowdrops out for three weeks and, more recently, of violets and iris stylosa; the rectory garden is rather too high and exposed for that to happen. Finally, all around me, I noticed signs of the search for food; rather mysterious and exciting. Beneath the conifers were fir cones eaten almost to a skeleton by squirrels. The compost heap showed the usual signs of scavenging by blackbirds and thrushes, but what about that penetrating hole? Could it have been a rat after a piece of apple peel?

FEBRUARY

IT IS DIFFICULT not to comment on the prevailing weather. A national daily showed a photo the other day of boys of Magdalen College School, Oxford canoeing across their cricket ground. Looking down upon Bodiam I saw that their cricket and rugger ground was almost entirely flooded and the Castle Inn seemed isolated among the waters which covered many acres.

On the Newenden cricket ground deep long-on or deep third man (dependent on the bowling end) would have had water well over their ankles. Nearby Selmes' Meadows were three quarters flooded and the farmer had moved his sheep to higher ground. Ploughed land near the old mill at Iden Green had become a lake and two herons were standing sentinel on the edge, outwardly relaxed but alert for the frog or fish exploring exciting new waters.

Birds are amazingly quick to use and enjoy flooded farmland and a typical example of this has been seen most days this week where the Rolvenden road crosses the Hexden channel; one day several hundred black-headed gulls and lapwings were joined by a few common gulls and a dozen or so rooks and, as with all wildlife, such gatherings mean congenial conditions and food. And still the rain descends. But take heart – this week we celebrated the feast day of Candlemas and connected with it is an old country rhyme:

"If Candlemas day be fair and bright,
  Winter will have another flight;
  If on Candlemas day it be shower and rain,
  Winter is gone and will not come again."

It rained, of course, so the second part is relevant.

Meanwhile, there has been a tiny touch of spring. Hazel catkins have lengthened an inch in five days, snowdrops are flowering in the garden and the grass is growing. I am slightly smug about this – my mower came back from its winter overhaul last week; all the same, I shall hold off as long as I possibly can.

Although rainfall has lessened this past week (only 5mm), it is significant that in this region small flooded areas of field are not receding, meaning of course, that at long last the water table must be up to near normal. A small plantation of cricket bat willows near the railway line has been standing in water since Christmas. Winter wheat will not like these conditions for long and cultivated turf even less so, as for example at Newenden where the low-lying centre of a field has turned brown.

MANY of us face February with trepidation. We dare also to think that it is Winter's last chance, remembering some hopeful words – "Much

LAPWING
by Winifred Austen RI, RE, FZS

February snow a fine summer doth show" Words of cheer for all of us but especially for the elderly and the housebound, who suffered in this recent very cold spell but conversely are uplifted by the thought of warmth and sun. Snow always brings variety to our daily routine and is a leveller; it tests our resilience, our courage and our ingenuity. Ditto in respect of wildlife. So birds and mammals come closer and are more bold. Most people, therefore, would have seen an influx on or near their bird-tables, including strangers such as waxwings, spotted woodpeckers and, in our case, herring gulls and rooks.

Several friends have reported the tracks of foxes round the house, testing dustbins and compost heaps. Quite shy birds like snipe can even appear on a lawn and two took flight off a frozen dyke on the Rother Levels one afternoon when the cold wind was so intense that I could not look ahead to check on the dog, so painful was it to the eyes. Driving through a copse the next morning, I slowed up for a lethargic woodcock, a slight rarity these days and unusual to see on the ground, except when probing for earthworms and insects.

That champion marauder, the woodpigeon, reacts energetically to snow. A flock of at least 200 were present last week on Old Place fields Sandhurst, vigorously attacking the tender green oil-seed rape through about three inches of snow. This ravaging of crops seems to go on all through the year until corn harvest and must be part cause for the ever-increasing numbers and the woodpigeon's label as the British farmer's greatest enemy. The rabbits, on the other hand, seem to give up in the face of snow and stay underground, living on their 'humps' or a few green shoots near their burrows.

It was pleasing, too, to see the revival of the snowman. Many exuded a personality, usually through headgear and muffler, and a few were inveterate pipe-smokers, trying thereby to keep warm! One large one, with ears, stood sentinel, as it were, right beside a 'sleeping policeman' across the lane behind us. Somewhere else in the area I saw a series of small snowmen lining a path to the front door in the manner of a guard of honour at a wedding.

Fortunately the cold spell has kept growth in check. Snowdrops and crocuses are now becoming more general in gardens but very few clumps of hazel catkins are evident and I have yet to see any pussy willow. The church weather-vane pointed south-west last night and Mr. Ron Lobeck forecast rain, so let us hope that February 'fill-dyke' will even now operate. It will also bring my rain-gauge into action, after looking like an outsize ice-cream cornet all through the snow.

SNOWY weather has its compensations. It draws family and friends closer round the fire. It also draws animals and birds closer to human habitation. So reports of shy birds coming close to the house have flowed in. One friend has had at least two kingfishers enjoying her bacon fat some five yards from her window, whilst another had the equally exciting sight of blackcaps, male and female, feeding off his bird-table. A rarity indeed, since the few that do winter here are normally in south-west England or Ireland; most blackcaps are in the southern Mediterranean or equatorial Africa. Longtailed tits have been seen on at least two bird-tables, snipe were feeding in the field behind Oaks Forstal, two visitors came across an eider duck at Rye Harbour and a whole crowd of mallard have recently been residing on the rectory ponds.

Last week, too, a robin landed confidently on the car roof, inches from where I stood in the garage. Such is the effect of frost and snow. But I suppose one worries more about wrens, tree-creepers and song thrushes which feed almost exclusively on insects; the RSPB expects the death toll of these species to be the highest since the freeze-up of 1962-3. I was delighted, therefore, to see yesterday (with the snow gone) a lively wren in my garage and a tree-creeper working its way up the nearest conifer. But an even better sight came later in the day driving down Newenden hill – numerous rooks busily refurbishing their nests in the copse on the left. Spring is definitely round the corner.

THIS morning I stood once again in the lambing shed at Hoad's Farm, Sandhurst. It was a reassuring sight. As usual, it spoke of the continuing cycle of the countryside and of fertility. It reminded me of that well-known verse in Genesis "While the earth remaineth, seedtime and harvest, and cold and heat, and summer and winter, and day and night shall not cease."

About 100 Suffolk ewes, who had been with a Kent ram, were peacefully quartered there in the thick hay. One had recently given birth to twins, the result of the common practice of letting a ram run with the ewes which were barren the previous year. So far twelve lambs had arrived; the serious business would soon begin this month when about 900 ewes would, hopefully, give birth, all of them under cover near the farmhouse.

David, the shepherd, was in the process of administering a worm drench to a dozen specially penned ewes. Even to the layman's eye they all seemed in superb condition. My friend Jeremy, the farmer, confirmed this impression. Somehow the wet autumn had produced well-conditioned ewes who had benefited from continuing growth of grass. A farmer friend in Romney Marsh confirmed this even more strongly; in his case his sheep had also fed on kale and other green stuff and they were in better condition than he could ever remember.

Romney Marsh is to me the home of Kents and it

FEBRUARY FILL-DYKE
by Martin Hardie RWS, RSW, RE

is good to know that, on at least one farm, they are still the majority breed. My friend, Gordon, belongs to a family who has farmed on the Marsh for at least four generations. Some of his ewes have run with a three-quarter bred Suffolk ram but the majority with a Kent ram, thus ensuring that he always has his Kent ewes. He finished his chat with a good story illu-strating the wonder and fertility of Nature and the scientific advances in the farming world. A farmer friend had recently told him that, out of 428 ewes scanned, only eight were not 'in lamb', an amazingly small proportion, but he added "I am not com-pletely surprised; the ewes went to the ram quickly, a good sign."

From the romantic open-ness of Romney Marsh to the lowlands of Scotland and Roger and Susie, a husband and wife team, like so many these days. Their lambing had begun on January 7th and their difficulties had been compounded by "really hor-rendous gales", no snow, but four power failures in one week and no farm generator. It had been a physical and mental battle. Lambing had only been possible under cover in their weather-tight lambing shed, able to hold about 350 ewes at one time. It was not till January 26 that they had dared to let out nine 'single' Suffolk lambs into a nearby field. Susie was delighted to tell me of two Suffolks who had lost their lambs and were in each case given a twin from another ewe. Within three hours both mothers had accepted their adopted 'child', without the sub-terfuge of the original fleece.

BARN owls remain a talking-point. The RSPB thanking me for a small donation to their Barn Owl Appeal, tell me that the Society is carrying out a major study in Suffolk this winter. They are seeking to create and maintain grassland ideal for barn owls to feed on. Movements and feeding habits will be carefully monitored. Nevertheless, in contrast to the UK generally, this part of the Weald is remarkably well-off for this beautiful and distinctive bird. Within a five mile radius of Benenden there are at least three breeders of the owl and in the same area are five nesting pairs known to me. Intensive far-ming may still be with us but, alongside that, are increased areas of rough pasture through the 'set aside' scheme, in turn encouraging voles, field mice and shrews which barn owls need to survive.

MARCH

IT is St. David's Day, 1st March and, appropriately, early daffodils are in flower. One might say that the countryside and country dwellers are "holding their breath" – are we about to have an early Spring or not?

The lapwings who usually move off if severe weather is threatening are still around in large numbers in Romney Marsh and North Kent, as well as in the Weald. The rooks are frantically building their nests. On Lamberden Farm, Sandhurst there are now at least ten nests whereas two weeks ago there were none, all having been demolished by the great storm. Admittedly they are not the most refined of nests – sticks and mud, but the builders are still motivated by instinct as well as breeding energy.

The busy scene reminded me of myself in the early '60s living at Ivychurch Rectory, when I received from the Ministry of Agriculture a letter addressed to "All Rookery Owners", asking permission to cull some of the rooks who were so numerous as to be considered a nuisance to farmers. Times have changed. That year their nest-building and accompanying noise coincided with an early Easter on 2nd April and, sitting at my desk in full view of the rookery, I began my sermon with the words "With the urge to mate and build goes new hope and new pleasure in life . . ." Other nest-building is much less obvious, if begun at all. One pair of mistle-thrushes have certainly begun in this area and a pair of mallard are paddling around the rectory pond, quietly prospecting.

Then again there was hope in my favourite hedgerow – not a thick, high hedge but tangled and unkempt, made up of a medley of beech, oak and willow seedlings, interspersed with wild rose, broom and bramble, with rush grass fed by clear water flowing along the ditch. In that 200 yard stretch have appeared, in the depths, about 60 primrose plants carrying 30 or so flowers. It faces south and must be full of scent in the summer as it is alive with butterflies on a sunny day, mainly gatekeepers, meadow browns and common blues.

However, our bird-table on St. David's day still reflects Winter. With recent frosts and no rain the ground has hardened up and there is a strong NW wind blowing, with snow showers forecast. So there is quite a crowd. In one go I can count twelve species. Most attractive, I suppose, are the nuthatches whose sharp beaks scare the others away from the nut bag. But for sheer *joie de vivre* the blackbirds take the prize when they are tucking into the apple peelings.

A DAFFODIL WOOD
by Annie L. Pressland

AS MANY of us know, dogs are often good timekeepers. They appear to have built-in alarm clocks which go off at, say, two o'clock and demand that walk. Last week I experienced a curious case of a pair of Canada geese who for five consecutive mornings at or around 7.30 a.m. flew honking over the house, always in the same direction. The call of some water and feeding-ground must have been regular and strong.

A squashed frog in the lane reminds me of another call to water. Late February or early March the common frog and the common toad are on the move after hibernation in some muddy ditch, seeking their breeding pond. Toads especially are particular and often travel a mile or two, passing by apparently suitable ponds till they reach their choice, possibly where they were born. I think I remember reading in the past of such numbers crossing a country road that local conservationists had erected a temporary notice which read "Beware, toads crossing".

THE occasion is special. A cease-fire in the Gulf has suddenly taken place and the Commander of the British Forces has asked for England's church bells to be rung. So in at least two towers in the Weald, Sandhurst and Rolvenden, they were rung that very same night. Some of us who rang were conscious, perhaps, of doing something deeply traditional and historical and rather more linked with the country parish church than the town. Innumerable towers in Kent and Sussex must have sent signals and lit beacons, warning of the Spanish Armada. Many years later, the same towers will have been observation posts for our Home Guard in those memorable months of 1940 and then their bells will have rung joyfully for victory in 1945. Memories such as these will have come to Sandhurst's captain who rang for VE Day and VJ Day. So there were 'touches' of Grandsire and some crisp clear 'rounds', celebrating the majority view that good had once again overcome evil.

Meanwhile the vagaries of English weather have been active. In a fortnight the snow is almost forgotten and mild weather is with us. Hazel catkins are widespread and lengthening. Pussy willow is just appearing along the Rother and the pinks and reds of early camellias and rhododendrons are shyly showing in their buds. Moreover, a pair of mallard appeared yesterday in the field alongside our boundary, peering through the wire fence and obviously on a nesting reconnaissance. Beside them a blackbird had gathered up nesting material in its beak, stirred by the same instinct. Both birds are officially March nesters, but, given a few mild days, they can easily begin in January or February. A few gardeners have been enticed out this week, mowers have gone into action (perhaps too hastily?) and in one vegetable garden I pass daily with the dog there has appeared a newly sown row, maybe of lettuce or broad beans.

THE blackthorn has lived up to its reputation. A week of north winds, snow and frost (worse in the rest of the country) has halted the countryside in its tracks. Dog walkers have had to be prepared for anything – a snow flurry, sunshine or just cold greyness, all within one hour. Those harbingers of stormy weather, the gulls, have been descending upon the field behind us in numbers – one morning about 70, doing their usual curious 'patrolling' and only occasionally picking something up. Another morning they finished with a ten minute conference, 30 in a tight circle, exchanging news and views, perhaps on ploughing in the locality or the delicacies on the nearest refuse dump. In the garden the daffodils have been broken or flattened, the early camellias have turned brown and the bird-table been surrounded by a squabbling crowd of all sizes, with a few rooks and jackdaws on the fringes. Within that crowd have been a pair of blackbirds simply revelling in my apple peelings, and what gentlemen they are, compared with the starlings, wide-boys one and all.

I SEEK once more to recommend a pre-breakfast walk – even in March. It fills the lungs with fresh air and blows away the cobwebs. It has its own special atmosphere of uncertainty, of excitement even. Today at 7 a.m. I have a white frost at my feet and above me a clear blue-grey sky. The few noises are country. As Oliver and I leave the field and move down our lane, we hear the harsh 'kronk' of a heron and watch two fly over our heads, slowly and leisurely, to some nearby pool. A minute later, two Canada geese headed south towards the Rother honking loudly, their wing-beat strong and steady like some cross-channel swimmer. As a contrast, numerous gulls flapped silently, a hundred feet up, almost floating and then suddenly decided to dip down onto our field for their morning snack and daily conference. The most noise came from the Frensham Manor rookery over the way where there was tremendous activity as well. The experts state that they have 'a wide vocabulary' and re-furbishing their nests seems to bring out the full width. There are the small sounds as well and without fail we stop and listen to the tiny stream as it wanders off the fields and under the lane, finally to end in Hexden Channel. All this, just a glimpse of the joys of an early morning stroll.

Such feelings emerge continually in TV's 'Country Ways' on a Monday evening. The programme may present country life as idyllic and always summer but invariably the people interviewed are deeply content and happy. They see

THE THORN TREE
by C. Conway Plumbe

their animals as their friends. The husband and wife at Nonington in the Lydden Valley declared "we adore our calves and two milking cows, Buttercup and Emma. It may sometimes be cold and muddy but we love the life". Their eyes and those of the others are truly open and their senses tuned to the smells and colours and noises around them. Those people have no wish to live anywhere else or go anywhere else for interest and entertainment. Some, perhaps many, may not go regularly to church but I suspect that they personify the creature communicating with the Creator.

I have noticed considerable ploughing since Christmas. It is not surprising. An unusually wet autumn delayed many farmers. In addition, there are incentives. Dare I say it – cereal farmers have not had it so good for a long time! Provided they set aside 15% of their land, they can claim a very worthwhile subsidy per acre of wheat grown. Further, prices are at their highest since Black Wednesday when the £ plummetted. So all is not gloom on the farming front, whatever farmers may say.

GARDENERS may have noticed that grass, whether rough pasture or lawn, has been growing in the past few weeks. Sheep have continued to graze and farmers have had to feed less hay than usual. Soil temperature must have been above average. Above average also have been the flocks of lapwings this winter. Sometimes statuesque on grass, but other times soaring and plunging in great flocks of 200 or more, as found near Iden Grange, Staplehurst. Numbers of the same species of a bird can vary, too, within Kent. A farmer friend below the North Downs near Hythe reports a distinct lack of fieldfares and redwings, yet in these parts I see and hear about large flocks, above average, as for instance in the Tubbslake area, near Hawkhurst.

Canada geese seem to be on reconnaissance at the moment. Early today I woke to a grand sight – a flight of nine in V formation passed only a few feet above the house, honking loudly. It is to me a stirring sound, evocative of marsh and estuary and the next moment I always expect to hear the high-pitched alarm call of the redshank.

APRIL

I CAME across an impromptu game of cricket on the first day of April. It was a lovely day, sunny and warm, and I suddenly found it on the lawn of a house due to be the centre for a christening lunch the next day. It was purely family, of course. Aunt Sarah was batting (with an ancient bat) and having to hit a croquet ball and to penetrate two very young, energetic fielders, especially Richard aged 5, who in his blue tracksuit threw himself around in all directions and showed great potential. Father lobbed up a slow ball to the batsman from time to time, whilst mother contented herself by standing out of range and carrying in her arms Arabella, aged 3. Also out or range was their Jack Russell, snuffling in the undergrowth. I was also granted family status and allowed a bowl and later a bat. The bat stung and, the croquet ball being rather heavy, I concentrated on glancing it to leg! Edmund Blunden, the Kent poet, to whom cricket was "as the air one breathed", would have thoroughly approved.

EVEN A remote country church has its day. In the case of All Saints, Ulcombe that might well have been 2nd April. The occasion was the inauguration of the new High Sheriff of Kent, the chief officer of the Crown in the county. To the historian and the traditionalist everything must have seemed right.

Into this lovely and tastefully arranged church came colour and ceremony and some of the leading officials in Kent. Trumpeters from the Coldstream Guards, in their bearskins, heralded the procession as they entered – outgoing and incoming High Sheriffs and their chaplains, with the Presiding Judge, supported by the Chief Constable, the Chairman of Kent County Council, the Mayor of Maidstone and their respective officers.

It was a far cry from those Norman builders of All Saints, who might have begun with a simple nave and small chancel and later installed a few monks to say Mass and staff the Collegiate church. They might have lived in the original part of Ulcombe Place next door and worked the farm on the other side of the church. Long years ago, at least two others from Ulcombe had been High Sheriffs. But the prize for longevity belong to two magnificent yews in the churchyard, one 1,000 years old and the other possibly 3,000! Beside such antiquity, sniffer dogs and terrorist bombs are a pale passing shadow.

APRIL 10th was an exciting day. I saw my first brood of young mallard, nine strong, following mother across the rectory pond. Later I saw my first brimstone butterfly of the season and my first cricket match – a serious group of young boys, two

APRIL SUNSHINE AFTER RAIN
by Martin Hardie RWS, RSW, RE

properly padded, on St. Michael's recreation ground; as usual, a dispute was in the process of being settled. That same day others saw their first swallow, at St. Ronan's School, a pleasure still in store for me; a moment too when I always marvel at the strength of that small body and the mystery of the homing instinct. The next day, 11th, I and others in Sandhurst heard the cuckoo and we knew that spring was really present. Indeed April is an exciting month, as Robert Browning certainly felt in his famous poem beginning

"Oh, to be in England
Now that April's there . . ."

Everywhere one looks there is new life and movement and, with it, new hope – ranging from the delicate lady's smock in the ditch to the crimson camellia by my study window and the watchful blackbird on her nest by the potting shed. This week, too, a rabbit crossed my path, its mouth overflowing with hay, presumably to line its burrow – all part of the same urge. But yesterday I beheld the sight that above all belongs to April, a cherry tree in blossom. I find myself at one with A. E. Houseman in his words from A Shropshire Lad -

"Loveliest of trees, the cherry now,
Is hung with bloom along the bough,
And stands about the woodland ride
Wearing white for Eastertide."

A LATE Easter Day is imminent and we are about to remove our bird-table to its summer shelter in our small barn. For some days now the house sparrows have been in the majority and one knows then that the time has come. We must stop feeding the birds. Natural food is becoming available and mating and nesting are increasingly No.1 priority. It is interesting to look back at the winter feeding season at the bird-table. Pride of place goes to our greater spotted woodpecker, resplendent in its crimson under-tail coverts, who patronised our nutbag for a week or two after the snow period; our nuts also went down rapidly from the powerful pointed bills of at least four nuthatches who seemed to be around all the winter and were a delight to observe, with their spruce blue-grey plumage and restless activity.

Besides them, we welcomed the usual variety of species, with titmice prominent; not more than the occasional thrush and only one or two greenfinches and sometimes a moorhen up from the pond. A more recent daily visitor has been a young small grey squirrel who became more and more at home sampling titbits on the ground. Like the birds, I view its presence with mixed feelings.

Easter Day also introduces the period for holding the Easter Vestry. Somehow this annual meeting continues to have more meaning and wider implications in country parishes. Held in the past in the parish church vestry, any resident whether churchgoer or not, Non-conformist or Jew, could attend and help elect the churchwardens for the ensuing year, and this still applies. Churchwardens continue to have legal status. Before any form of State Aid became available towards the end of the last century, one of their recognised duties was the collection and apportioning of alms to the sick and poor of the parish, as well as running the day-to-day affairs of their village. As a continuing emphasis on their legal status, churchwardens still have to be sworn into office by the archdeacon. In addition, an occasional churchwarden fulfils the modern role of overseer and is chairman of the parish council and a borough councillor.

YESTERDAY Oliver and I set out for our walk in a raw north-easterly wind. We had some shelter from a hedge but I envied him his closeness to the ground. Before long I saw my first bluebell of the season, at the foot of the hedge on the sunny side. Also nearby and flowering early was a patch of greater stitchwort, so called because the plants were thought to cure a 'stitch' – a pain in the side of the body. Many is the time in my schooldays that I could have done with that cure!

But there was more early spring flowering. Below this same hedge, on the bank above the water-level of the ditch, were several stems of lady's smock in flower, pale and delicate. Maybe in June these same flowers will have on them the whitish yellow eggs of the orange-tip butterfly. In the hedge above were numerous clusters of oak-apples. These, of course, are caused by gall wasps. They insert their eggs into an oak shoot and these strange protuberances, known as galls, result. But this is only a tiny part of the picture. Even in winter a large oak supports a wealth of life beneath its bark, to say nothing of the grey squirrel's drey in the crown or the fox's earth beneath its roots. Back to reality though – Oliver had had the same thought. He was deep in the bank under the hedge, only hind-quarters and tail visible, soil flying in all directions. He was obviously happy and warm; I was not, so I turned for home

A HOLIDAY in the Highlands of Scotland was bound to be a contrast to the Weald of Kent. Scenery, farming, way of life – were all different which is one of the joys of a holiday. There were surprises, too, one of them being initially when staying near the centre of Edinburgh. Our friends had a pocket handkerchief of a garden, but it contained ducks, chickens, bantams, a goose and a 'pond'; my friend, Robin, is clearly a countryman at heart. Later we experienced the grandness and loneliness of Sutherland. The people must surely exist on fishing, sheep and tourism and keep themselves warm with peat in winter.

The village of Scourie seemed typical. White-

KENTISH CHERRY BLOSSOM
by E. H. Adie BWS

washed houses huddled round a first-class fisherman's hotel and one all-purpose shop where the Royal Mail called once a day to disembark and collect passengers as well as letters. At a council house opposite lived the Registrar of Births, Marriages and Deaths, whose Hours of Business were announced as "Weekdays: any reasonable hour". A church, a camping site and a tiny harbour (deserted except for four rowing boats) completed the picture. But, of course, always along that rocky north-west coast there were the sea birds and the seals; the latter, as usual, played hide and seek with our young boatman who was both naturalist and seaman. Also of course there were other things like Scottish pancakes and castles and tweeds, which all contributed towards a memorable holiday. Taking all-in-all, quite heady fare.

LAST week I shared in a delightful Week of Arts and Crafts in the tiny village of Wormshill hidden away on the North Downs. Encouraged by Maidstone Borough Council, the villagers of all ages enjoyed themselves learning and experimenting in the realms of music, painting, pottery, flowers and needlework. New interests and talents were found, horizons enlarged. Saturday brought the climax of a procession and a play. Civic leaders with badges and official headgear followed the players, all in their teens, some with home-made banners, through the leafy main street and churchyard to the Village Hall. Here we all relaxed in the open air and the sunshine for the drama, a play devised by the young about their patron saint St. Giles, patron of cripples, beggars and blacksmiths! Opening scenes presented Druids planning the annual sacrifice of a child to appease the gods; consternation among the villagers was suddenly transformed by the appearance of St. Giles in their midst and the rescue of the sacrifice. Delightful and natural. The only props, a home-made backcloth and a drum, a tambourine and two recorders, lending a little tension or joy as required. Real rural England.

MAY

IT IS always an education to stand still outside one's front door at midnight. The night yields noises that are both familiar and mysterious. Around you, too, are shapes that puzzle and almost threaten. In front of me stood the great oak silhouetted against a patch of light night sky, made momentarily brilliant by a flash of lightning, followed by a distant thundery rumble. Into the ensuing silence came the harsh penetrating 'kr-r-kr' of a moorhen on the pond, a bundle of nervous energy, head and tail jerking, always on the move even after dark. A little further off a lamb was calling for its mother and the 'hoo-hoo-hoo' of two tawny owls floated over from Silverden wood. At my feet among the St. John's Wort a slight rustling proclaimed the presence of a field mouse, searching perhaps for a half-forgotten stockpile of berries. Last but not least, sounds of munching told me that our chestnut mare was grazing near the orchard fence, typical of most horses who seem to feed all night. All this, evidence of much nocturnal activity by countless wild creatures. What greater dividends would a silent vigil in some wood produce!

A HOLIDAY by car inevitably brings new landscapes. I suppose that the most stirring of these was the Pennines, with strips of snow still showing here and there against the backcloth of the dark peaty soil. Around us the only sign of movement seemed to be from blackfaced sheep and their lambs and one lonely pony, not far from the Cat and Fiddle Inn, said to be the highest licensed premises in England.

What a contrast it was to drop down into Buxton with its Georgian facades and air of elegance and culture. But the end of our journey was Lincolnshire which gives, in the south, the widest possible views of earth and sky as well as farming on a grand scale. Nevertheless my thoughts the next day went to the Wolds and Somersby (Tennyson's birthplace) and my friend Peter, who is rector of ten parishes there (total population about 800!).

It was obvious at once that he was a round peg in a round hole. He clearly loved his spacious Regency rectory with its view, its garden and its outbuildings, and he insisted on a tour of inspection. Accompanied by a labrador and springer spaniel we inspected two goats (one being milked by his wife), two ferrets, numerous guinea fowl, chicken and rabbits and twelve calves, belonging to a local farmer. In the garden were two long rows of early potatoes, a broad herbaceous border and a cock pheasant calling from the copse. "What more can I ask for?" he said. A true country parson.

GREENHEDGES FARM
by *Martin Hardie* RWS, RSW, RE

LAST night St. George's Church in the middle of Romney Marsh welcomed a contemporary George, none other than the newly consecrated Archbishop of Canterbury. The occasion was Evensong and the Archbishop's first Visitation to any deanery in his diocese. The Marsh people were thrilled and flocked into this grand medieval church at Ivychurch, possibly the finest complete example of 14th century architecture and craftmanship in the county. Almost 400 people came to greet and listen to their new bishop, undoubtedly the largest congregation in the history of that church.

The Marsh had already worked its magic on me by the time he arrived. Miles of grazing sheep and lambs stretched from Appledore to Snargate and a heron was still probing a dyke near Vinal Farm. Parking my car under the Rectory rookery, I recalled a letter I had received, years ago, from the Ministry of Agriculture, addressed to "All Rookery Owners". A junior clergyman and yet a landowner on the Ministry mailing list! Nearby a donkey was grazing, quite oblivious of cars or the importance of the occasion, and beyond lay the rectory pond, alleged to contain the finest leeches in Romney Marsh!

So to the church and its battlemented porch, walking up a brown carpet (surely it should have been red?), which covered its uneven but truly rural brick path. Inside, the large church was already half full, with 45 minutes still to go, the Southlands School orchestra tuning up, the bells being chimed, children squatting on the steps of the font (where my own two were christened) and the sidesmen already looking anxious about seating.

Finally, the moment came and the procession moved up the long, lofty church – "All people that on earth do dwell, Sing to the Lord with cheerful voice . . ." At the rear, of course, the Archbishop in the cope and mitre of his enthronement with its modern Pentecostal design. "In the name of the Lord we greet you" said the Rural Dean and we all moved into the rhythm and cadences of Prayer Book Evensong still, thank God, familiar to most and much loved by many. Strictly, the sermon is an appendage, but the climax for some. Not unexpectedly, the Archbishop was simple yet theological, the ideal, with words like 'glory' and 'joy' being stressed in this Ascensiontide address.

Occasionally my attention wandered and I recalled, years ago, the faithful 8 or 10 who worshipped there Sunday by Sunday, mostly farming folk, supported once a month by a string quartet from this tiny village. What a contrast with this evening! Yet what a reward for that faithful few! In some ways, though, the climax came in the recessional hymn "Rejoice the Lord is King", expressing so suitably, one hoped, the thoughts of that great gathering. One hoped also that some had read the oval textboard over the door, recording Jacob's feelings after his dream "How dreadful is this place! This is none other but the house of God". Should that not be the reaction of every individual; a little fear, a little mystery and, most important, the sense of a Presence?

IT WAS sunny with a north wind and our third day on holiday on the Cornish coast. Our destination was St. Anthony Head and its lighthouse, standing on the point of a sparsely populated peninsula. A lonely station, but not as bad as some. When we rang, there was a surprise. The door was opened by a woman. It was a man and wife team - one of three in the Trinity House circuit. Fortunately it was fully automatic, so they could go to bed at night without worry.

Retracing our steps we paused in the tiny village of Gerrans, complete with the usual white-washed houses surrounding pub, church and chapel. We ventured into the church and my glance caught the War Memorial of Cornish slate and, seemingly, warm to the touch. I was fascinated and saddened by what I saw. One hundred and eighty had died in the First World War – why there were scarcely 100 houses in the village now! Four only had died in the last war; thank God for humanitarian leadership!

Later in the day we took the footpath from St. Mawes to St. Just along Newton Cliff, owned, we were glad to see, by the National Trust. The view was, to say the least, impressive. Below us a choppy sea, with Falmouth nestling into the hills across the bay. Riding at anchor in Carrick Roads were eight Russian factory ships, waiting for the local boats to unload their catch. A great crowd of gulls surrounded one of them and two cormorants skimmed the waves heading out to sea. Beneath our feet, a wide stretch of grass bordered by gorse, and the wind whistling round our ears. This was suitable habitat for coastal birds and before long we sighted a rock pipit and a stonechat.

We returned eventually to St. Mawes, invigorated and a little tired. Lingering on the quayside, we found shelter from the wind and the calmness that comes with evening. The resident grebe was playing hide and seek in the harbour bay, a sanderling was looking for morsels at the water's edge and one large gull was successfully contesting a discarded sandwich with three interested but hesitant rooks.

OUR rectory pond is at its best at the end of May and early June. However small a piece of water, there is always something happening and different from yesterday. Around and beneath the surface of every pond, natural or man-made, there is life, vigorous but often unseen. Small wonder that most passers-by up the Bodiam road stop and look or that the village young use its railings from time to

THE KINGCUP DELL
by Theresa S. Stannard

time as their gathering place.

At the moment the willows, many low and twisted, are at their greenest; the abundant yellow iris give a gentle colourful surround, tinged at the rear by some purple rhododendrons planted by a pre-war rector, Canon Beale; a lovely clump of kingcups, astride the inflow from the old strawberry fields, have just died away. On the water itself are two families of mallard, contending with the usual predators and the hazards of crossing the road to the larger piece of water opposite, but loving the privacy and security of our plentiful reeds. Moorhen come and go but none are nesting and they appear to have yielded the territory to the mallard for the summer.

Beneath the surface are a fair number of fish, probably tench which, when young, feed readily on the algae which forms on the water from time to time. Sadly I have not seen any frogs for a year or two, although in the past small boys have put tadpoles from elsewhere into our pond; but so few survive to the frog stage as they form main food for other pond creatures. Last week, though, I heard some marsh frogs, as opposed to the common frog, at Smallhythe and in the river at Newenden, truly living up to their Latin name 'ridibunda', meaning 'laughing'. A few of these in the rectory pond might give quite a shock to the late-night reveller returning home on foot!

Last but not least, the pond is a permanent source of moisture to our garden and woodland birds. Being fed by spring, as well as surface water from field and road, it never dries up and its level does not alter a lot, even in the 1976 drought. A few weeks ago the occasional swallow and house martin were skimming the water to drink or landing for a moment on the muddy edge to collect mud for their nest-building. All this a microcosm of the vigorous life in and around one pond. How fortunate we are in the Weald to possess so many, quite a few of them survivals from old iron-ore workings. They are part of our rich inheritance and deserve sensible care from owners and communities.

JUNE

WOULD I arrange a bellringers' outing to Romney Marsh? I did not need asking twice! Rich in history and churches and a special landscape beauty, the area draws me like a magnet. Our first stop was Lympne, church and castle side by side on the ridge, where I grew up and learned to ring, and full of memories. We used their new ringing chamber on the first floor and later inspected the belfry – most of it new, except for the bells and mostly installed by their own members – a credit to craftsmanship and enthusiasm. The bells were smooth if a little noisy. A few of us climbed to the very top of the tower. What a view in spite of distant rain!

Now, down to the Marsh, across the Royal Military Canal and the Hythe to Dungeness railway, to New Romney church, built by the Normans on the harbour quayside, a landmark to the sailors and a proclamation of the Christian message. The eight bells here were a good test for accurate striking and we only ventured touches of Grandsire and Bob Major on the 'back 6'. After tea and talk we retraced our steps to Burmarsh, a tiny church with a light ring of six; beside it "The Shepherd and Crook" and sheep grazing the churchyard only as it should be. As a contrast Newchurch was very large, built on higher ground, undoubtedly a refuge for the whole community from flood, storm and foreign marauder. Its six bells, rehung in 1969, went well but we still failed over Bob minor. In spite of this a good half day for all eleven ringers and, I hope, our four supporters. As usual we were welcomed at each tower and were very grateful for permission to ring.

THE country parson's day is not what it was. My grandfather, rector of Bicknor and Hucking on the North Downs before the first war, invariably managed two or three hours a day in his garden. Not surprisingly he won prizes for his violets and orchids. If not in his greenhouse he might be on his way to Maidstone Market in pony and trap to give an opinion on someone's cattle or to lead an expedition of the Kent Archaeological Society. In spite of this he knew his people whose interests anyway were mainly his.

In contrast I managed yesterday a rare pleasure – a day in the garden! Preparing the ground for some late new potatoes I was soon joined by a blackbird. No fear, just concentrating on the job in hand – feeding his young. One, two, three, four worms in his beak, and yet another, all sizes and wriggling. Away he went into the nearby bush and within seconds was back on my hoe and collecting another five worms. What a life! The potatoes in, I set the

THE CATTLE MARKET
by Edith M. Garner

motor-mower in action, to be given a pleasant surprise. Two early purple orchids stood on the lower lawn, a little stunted, but not surprisingly, as they had grown since the last cut, nine days before. Quite an achievement. This discovery drove me into the paddock and yet another early purple greeted me, flowering for the first time since I removed the plant from Newenden hill two years ago, just before a lorry-load of soil would have been tipped on top of it. Strictly illegal but the right thing, I thought, in the circumstances

LAST week, as a countryman, I seemed to enjoy an abundance of wild-life and conservation matters. It began with a quite outstanding pre-sale viewing at Christie's of the contents of Charles Tunnicliffe's studio, followed the next day by the issue of four beautiful butterfly stamps, and completed on Sunday by the BBC's cameras spending all day at Minsmere in Suffolk.

Christie's was a unique occasion. Charles Tunnicliffe was described in The Field as "the greatest bird and wildlife artist in Britain this century" and there, spread over four large rooms, were the contents of his studio – measured drawings, watercolours, manuscripts and, above all, sketchbooks; a privilege indeed; one didn't know where first to begin or look. Almost all his drawings were interestingly inscribed, too, e.g. "Goldfinch.

Obtained from T. G. Walker, Henblas, Anglesey. About March 28th 1946. This bird found dead on the road by one of Mrs Walker's scholars..." Nevertheless, if I had had several thousand pounds spare, I would have bought one of his sketchbooks – spontaneous, warm, life-like. Yet, as it turned out, the sale never took place. The Isle of Anglesey Council bought the whole lot for £400,000 two days before. If Tunnicliffe's works are a national heritage, I suppose this was right.

Then those beautiful butterfly stamps. Congratulations to the Post Office and Gordon Beningfield, the artist, who took infinite trouble to portray accurately the large blue and the chequered skipper in spite of their being probably extinct in England. Both are almost certainly victims of modern farming methods; agricultural sprays have destroyed their natural habitat and food. Finally, on Sunday, most skilful photography produced some exciting glimpses at Minsmere which is perhaps the most notable success of the RSPB. Unexpected was the sight of an osprey diving for fish and, even more so, the attack, seconds later, by a marsh harrier. A pair of these latter are, I believe, resident in the Rother valley between Bodiam and Newenden.

NATURE is full of surprises. One came to us a week ago as my wife opened up the long box containing our croquet set at the back of the garage.

To her amazement she found it filled with broken dog biscuits and sacking. Reflection told us that a very busy rat had been at work. It had removed, from a 25 lb. bag near the garage door, about 4 lbs. of biscuit and handfuls of sacking, presumably to make a comfortable nest with store cupboard nearby. One longed to know more – particularly how long it had taken to do it. My friend Ernie, experienced countryman and rodent operator, had never seen anything like it. The only comparable experience for me occurred some ten years ago when a mouse had completely filled an empty jam jar in the rectory larder with soft material and small broken dog biscuits. The same instinct, presumably, of providing a comfortable nest and plenty of food.

It was reassuring to read in the paper the other day that the black or ship rat, the carrier of the bubonic plague, is almost extinct in this country. That might be the one credit mark for the larger, more aggressive brown rat which gradually drove its cousin from SE Asia back to the ports of the UK.

WHATEVER the weather nowadays, June continues to be a favoured month for weddings and this also means that bellringers are kept busy. But three Sundays ago a band were ringing long and expertly for a small baby, David Mathew Lewis. Both parents being ringers, various friends from Kent came together at Staplehurst to ring a three hour peal of over 5,000 changes in the Rutland method during the actual christening, which was supported in the church by more ringers. Such is the strength of telepathic communication, David is surely bound to be a ringer!

That same week, taking a party round Brenzett church in Romney Marsh, I referred to a less orthodox bellringer. My friend Basil was a long-serving churchwarden there, also builder-cum-undertaker throughout the Marsh. Every Sunday he handled the three bells in the belfry with skill and nonchalance – one rope in the left hand, another in his right and the middle one, looped, activated by his foot. Having completed that duty, he then led the singing with his splendid baritone voice.

Being a true Marshman and countryman, Basil would have approved of the colony of bees in a cavity of the south wall. Like myself, he would have regarded them as a natural part of a cottager's home and garden, where there was always a hive or two. Indeed he may have known this colony, as it has been in the church wall for at least five years, only a yard from a blocked priest's door of Norman origin. Country instinct and my father combine to make me always treat bees with great respect and regard them as friends and allies, so I was delighted to inherit two colonies in Sandhurst rectory. Although they infiltrated the upper floors from time to time, we were never once stung in 22 years. Apiarists now

WATERMEADOWS
by H. Sylvester Stannard RA

have to contend with the verroa honey bee parasite. Perhaps the wild colonies will have greater resistance. There are few things more soothing than tea on the lawn with honey sandwiches.

ONE does not expect to see the signature of Royalty in the visitors' book of an isolated country church. But there it was – a simple "Charles", not once, but twice within the last three years, in Thurning Church, Norfolk. A privilege indeed, and no wonder. The interior exuded history, not so much the architecture as the furnishings. I was spell-bound, transported back two centuries.

One's attention was immediately drawn to the magnificent 18th century three-decker pulpit, with sounding board, and then to the imposing row of ten box pews of similar date, each for a particular household and identified by very old labels, proclaiming Lime Tree Farm, Roundabout Farm, Rookery Farm, Manor Farm (larger pew), the Hall (very large!), Rectory (smaller), and so on. At the west end were further box pews for the servants. Significantly, just inside the door was "the Rector's coachman", strategically placed for him to exit as soon as the service was over. The rest of the village took pot luck on the 18th century benches in the centre, men and boys on the right and girls on the left – a custom maintained into the 1920s. Hat pegs lined the men's side; costing £2-18s in 1840. A gem of unrestored Georgian furnishing.

Outside Thurning Church still stood the Victorian stable for the ponies and, for miles around, open fields of sugar beet, corn and oil seed rape, broken in one direction by a shimmering sea of blue – some fields of flax. What a welcome and lovely sight this crop is, in the Weald as well as in East Anglia. In the distance was Sall, a very small village with "the largest and most glorious church in the county". A magnificent nave, with lofty clerestory and perfect acoustics. So chairs were ready for an orchestral concert that evening and "O Lord, open thou our lips", gently intoned by my friend, carried easily to the flower arranger in the sanctuary, some 150 feet away.

JULY

I AM a little sad today. It has been lovely and warm and sunny but the hay behind the house is being baled. Each day for the past week I have enjoyed so much those loose rows of hay, gradually changing colour, altogether rather traditional, a survivor of the old-fashioned farming scene and methods, which now never allow one to gaze upon stooked corn. It is all immediately swallowed up by the combine and lifeless rows of straw are spewed out across the stubble. Here in my hayfield I could daily savour and share the ripening process. First, of course, came the reaper, followed within yards by a host of house-martins swooping low over the cut grass, like gulls behind the plough, to snap up those hundreds of tiny insects. The next morning, rather more sedately and noisily, came a crowd of our local rooks, who returned each breakfast time, checking for wireworms and seeds. They and numerous starlings also descended every time the hay was turned. And all this past week there has been the smell, sweet and 'powdery', pleasing to my nostrils but demoralising to many a hay-fever sufferer. Nevertheless, I'm sure my friend, Gordon, made some very good hay.

HOLIDAYS usually bring contrasts, not least in a change of scenery and the natural life existing in it.

We exchanged a Wealden rectory for a converted barn on a hillside in the Dordogne valley. The first impression, which grew as we journeyed south, was of the greater numbers of swallows and house martins breeding in France. Our first lunch in a deserted tree-lined square beside a small village church brought this home to me. Our car was surrounded by about 30 house martins zooming criss-cross through the trees in the manner of performing gymnasts doing a stunt. Wherever we stopped, it was the same story – great gatherings of both species on the wires or of young house martins protruding out of their nests under the eaves of the old houses of those many picturesque small towns along the Dordogne river. These tiny energetic birds obviously feel warmer and safer in France than in England. Having said this, I must add that bird life in the places and areas I journeyed did not seem very obvious or interesting, though, as I expected, I did see one or two buzzards.

The exciting things for me were the butterflies. This came home to me when we stopped for lunch in a wood clearing north of Perigueux. Sitting in a chair eating my bread and paté I realised that I had an absolute feast of butterflies within a few feet. With the same flora as one would find in Hemsted Wood, Benenden, there were at least eight different

A KENTISH GARDEN
by E. H. Adie BWS

species, and in some numbers – three varieties of fritillaries, meadow browns, gatekeepers and common blues. In Hemsted Wood I might have seen just a few meadow browns, gatekeepers and speckled woods. In the uncropped meadow beside our Dordogne barn the same varieties were to be seen, loving the long hours of hot sunshine which, of course, engenders the more prolific breeding than in our own, often chilly, damp countryside.

THE deeply stirring notes of the Last Post and Reveille had just died away – not on the parade ground but in a country churchyard. Beside the open grave the bugler, upright, motionless, immaculate in the uniform and white helmet of the Royal Marines and the group of mourners, struck equally still and silent by those notes; all of us paying our last tribute to Sam, till his death the second oldest living Marine. What memories, what thoughts! The Boer War and both world wars and finally a clergyman. What a contrast too, between the strife and danger of war and his retirement home (under the shadow of Rolvenden's church tower) as well as his last resting-place amid the marguerites and buttercups. Thank God for the traditional unchanging role of the countryside, offering peace and sunlight and community for tired folk "when the fever of life is over and our work is done".

But, of course, for most country folk their work is not done. Some are gathering a short hay crop, while others are picking strawberries, for which a short season is forecast. Or again, in the feathered world, there is bustle, but there is time apparently for a breather. Below my study window stands a stake supporting the sedum in our herbaceous border. It is seldom unoccupied. First, and typically, a spotted flycatcher, restless and fly-swotting, but has he a mate and a nest in the fork of some nearby tree? Then in succession a song thrush and a bullfinch, both *en route* to nests in the paddock hedge, a robin and a wren. How garden birds love these vantage points supplied them by methodical gardeners.

I HAVE been giving some thought recently to roadside verges. When on holiday in Suffolk I noticed that, except at danger points, the verges on minor roads did not appear to have been cut since spring, if then; understandably they were full of botanical interest – a sympathetic county authority, I thought. Then I came across an article entitled "Flora of the Margins" in the journal of the Suffolk Naturalists' Society. This informative study of five 50 yard sections of the road verges of the A12, south-west of Ipswich, revealed that on one section no less than 64 different species were found; it was also significant that the least number of species on any section was 37. A day or so later I stopped to walk the dog on a verge beside the A1 and was delighted to find a colony of at least a hundred six-spot burnet moths, resting on the grass stems; maybe their cocoons had been there all the winter, as there was plenty of clover and bird's foot for the caterpillars to feed on. One could say a lot more, but clearly our roadside verges are of considerable value and interest.

Visiting down Bourne Lane as darkness fell, I found that one resident enjoys the reassuring company of several glow-worms on the bank at "Pippins". Ignorance caused some research to be done. Apparently the light comes from the wingless female beetles, from the underside of the two end segments of the body. The male, which is not often seen, is more beetle-like. According to Gilbert White, the 18th century parson-naturalist, you can attract the males in through the window by burning a candle in a darkened room – if you live in a glow-worm neighbourhood, which perhaps ours is.

Finally, it rained on St. Swithin's day, 15th July. It has rained each day since. The old rhyme remains mysteriously and wonderfully correct.

EXACTLY three years ago I wrote "Village churches are ideal for weddings. They allow for the individual stamp, plenty of time and often a truly English setting". Such was the case last Saturday at St. George's, Benenden for the wedding of Marion and Matthew whom I was privileged to marry. The cricket had already begun and there could be no more English or traditional setting than Benenden Green, surrounded by church, school and houses.

Bride and father, in a vintage Lagonda, eventually turned the corner and the cricket paused in greeting, to allow the car free passage behind the bowler's arm. Immediately afterwards the batsman hit a very straight 4! So into the service and the opening hymn "I vow to thee, my country . . .", not the usual choice but understandable, since the bridegroom and best man were in the dress uniform of the Royal Artillery and had fought with distinction in the Gulf War. There followed the rhythm and poetry of Cranmer's incomparable English "for better, for worse: for richer, for poorer . . ." with the appropriate Guard of Honour of brother officers outside the church at the end of the service. The cricketers, let it be recorded, were not to be outdone. They eventually formed their own guard of honour with their bats as bride and 'groom passed the Memorial Hall (temporarily the cricket pavilion). Maybe they were conscious of their status. Benenden cricket, having begun in Hemsted Park, was first played on the Green in 1802 when "the good ordinary of the Bull Inn" was rated almost as important as the cricket. The great days came a little later, between 1825 and 1838 when Edward Wenman and Richard Mills of Benenden

SUMMER SHADOWS
by Martin Hardie RWS, RSW, RE

and Kent carried all before them. Buried in the churchyard, they would, I'm sure, have approved of all they saw that Saturday.

No wedding is complete without the reception, which was also truly rural, on the bride's father's farm, buried deep in a fold of Wealden countryside. The marquee stood welcoming, on a recently cut hay-field which continued to offer numerous bales for tired feet and those seeking fresh air and a breeze. As a slight contrast we enjoyed the fellow company of a rather famous TV cook, but our caterer stood firm and offered him quails' eggs and the most delicate cucumber sandwiches without flinching.

WHAT treasures our country churches are! It is good sometimes to visit alone and sit, just oneself and God. I did just that on Saturday at Smarden, one of the Wealden market towns licensed by Edward III. Before entering the church I was struck by the 1939-45 War Memorial – beautifully clean but, curiously, recording more names than World War I, including five women. It in fact spoke of terror and tragedy in that picturesque village – two land-mines wiping out in a flash two families, the Smalls and the Woods, country folk sharing the same "terror by night" (and day) as their London cousins. We need to remember them and others like them as the clock strikes eleven on Remembrance Sunday. And what a lovely tone St. Michael's clock

has, too; its 'quarters' could compete with any Cambridge college clock.

Still, I could not enter. A large polite notice on the door told me to shut it "so that the birds may not die of hunger or thirst" and reinforced the plea with an illustration of two long-tailed tits and a bumble bee. I was intrigued. Over the years, in churches, I have found starlings, swallows, wrens, robins and blue tits but never the long-tailed variety. Seated at last, with the silence broken only by the steady tick of the clock, I was conscious at once of the wide, open and high nave, crowned, as it were, by a most striking scissor-beam roof. At the far, east, end burned the sanctuary lamp; behind me stood a rocking-horse. Quite a contrast and yet complementary. Mystery and new life in the sacrament; creation and innocence linked in that lovely plaything. "Except ye become as a child . . ."

AUGUST

THE Best Kept Village competition is undoubtedly taking its normal course in our villages. Quite properly judges do not tell them in advance of any visit and normally aim for two in the course of the summer. I am quite sure that, on balance, this competition remains a good one but there can be unfortunate consequences. These were highlighted about two months ago in an article in *The Times* by Kerry Gill entitled "Jackboots on the village green". It produced several pithy letters, in the main agreeing and also expressing my own views. As one writer put it – the competition can result in villages being "turned into manicured municipal parks". This is partly due to the competition guidelines and partly due to some village activists reflecting urban attitudes. These are often not eradicated even by years of residence in a village or country environment.

The real countryman is shaped and fed by the deep roots of birth and long residence. The competition surely aims to encourage residents to have a pride in their village and to control and remove things that disfigure it – namely litter and rubbish, garish adverts, too many road and street signs. The judges, hopefully, look for passable footpaths, grass verges that invite the passing horse to crop and hedges that are cared for but not shaven.

Much more recently there was a further, extreme illustration of urban attitudes. A Dorset smallholder on family land, was subject to a complaint by neighbours for causing a "noise nuisance", namely the crowing of his cockerels. Fortunately, on appeal, the Crown Court judge found in his favour. Such noises are a natural background to country life and are a delight to many who cannot begin to tune in to the man-made cacophony of town life. Often these noises are seasonal or temporary – a rookery when nesting and mating are in full swing, a flock of ewes when separated from their lambs and a herd of bullocks when short of food and water, their respective reactions very human. For me it is a privilege to have house martins under the eaves, mallard fly in regularly for food and water and a snooze and marsh frogs croaking all night.

THE French invaders seem to have been repulsed. I refer not to Napoleonic times but to our buddleia. Normally in August it is populated by a moving, restless crowd of peacocks, red admirals and tortoiseshells. This year its long, mauve, scented spikes had been attracting almost entirely these "French-speaking" large whites, with only one or two natives. But these last two days we have

THE END OF THE DAY
by Bertha Stamp

returned to normality. Peacocks, red admirals and tortoiseshells are in the majority.

I am reminded of a similar invasion in, I think, 1947. A particular variety of the clouded yellow butterfly swept across the Channel, visible in many Kent gardens. A further phenomenon was their clearly defined landing-stage, which was a field near the golf-course at Barton-on-Sea, Hampshire. Here they landed and rested and, as I stood there, I marvelled. A two acre field was alive with hundreds of clouded yellows, and yet most years one sees only a few in Southern England, if that.

ENORMOUS round bales pulled by equally enormous tractors roar frequently past our house. It should be impossible for anyone in the Weald not to recognise that a new corn harvest is in full swing. Thank God for continuous dry sunny weather at a vital time. As often, there is a contrast. So many still on holiday, alongside a few working the longest hours of their year, and yet others on the farming front poised for their height of activity – the hop-picking, imminent and so particular to Kent.

The view on my dog walk this afternoon reflected the prevailing farming scene. From near Potman's Heath there streched several miles of arable, intersected by dykes; near me wavy rows of straw, further away several hundred round bales, which contrasted with two neighbouring fields, already harrowed and waiting for drilling with oil-seed rape; new seed for a new harvest. Away to my left towards the Tenterden railway, there was still standing corn and, beyond, a combine making its slow, dusty way through yet more. In the distance, the Smallhythe ridge with its vineyard, their harvest yet to come. Somehow, in this warm August sunshine, I felt I could not ask for greater pleasure visually and mentally; it also spoke of hard work, fertility and, of course, the beauty of the English farming countryside.

WENSLEYDALE in Yorkshire is a world away from the Weald of Kent. All around are open grassy hillsides dotted with black-faced Swaledale sheep and stone byres and beautifully clear streams feeding beautifully clear rivers. One of these was the Ure and a mile stretch at Bainbridge was my favourite walk on holiday. Nearly always there was a fisherman mid-stream casting his fly but for me it was amazing how many species of birds I saw in that relatively short stretch, and some of them waders too, itself surprising, considering we must have been at least 60 miles from the nearest coast.

One typical day I disturbed on the track in front, two wheatears and further on, in bushes by the water, a crowd of redstarts. Flying up river were a pair of oystercatchers and standing sentinel on a nearby stone wall one of several redshank, calling the alarm note (were there young in the grass below?). A hundred yards further on were some common sandpipers flying from rock to rock and a black-headed gull with a broken wing and therefore only able to swim. And along the whole length there were innumerable wagtails, pied, grey and yellow, intermingling with swallows and martins, a scene exuding activity and *joie de vivre*.

SCARECROWS are seldom seen these days, modern devices having often displaced them. Nevertheless, all this summer I have enjoyed the company of two, full of character, guarding my daughter's large vegetable garden. One is an elegant lady, with a red top and all curves, keeping watch over the lettuce, tomatoes and sweet corn, and the other a large rotund man, obviously a beer drinker, threatening any birds daring to attack the spinach and greens. Whether effective or not, they give character to the whole garden and a sense of company as one digs up the potatoes. An ex-farmer friend, travelling by train up to London, suddenly saw "an extremely nice scarecrow" in the middle of a field of brassicas near Swanley. Dressed in blue, with a strong figure and hard hat, he looked very like Pc Plod, he said. Very appropriate.

ONCE more it was the County Show. A fine sunny day, but not too hot. There was the usual struggle to get through the crowd near the entrance, some mesmerised by the 'popular', non-agricultural stands, ranging from leather goods and men's fashions to kitchen gadgets. With concentration and perseverance one can quickly penetrate to the heart of the Show. In the cattle shed I improved my knowledge of the Dexter breed – average height 30 inches and 6 cwt. in weight, and, not surprisingly, some of the owners women, including a parson's wife. What a contrast they were to the Charolais further over and the Limousin, both so enormous that one wondered how they loaded the beasts for transit without special apparatus.

Next door, with the sheep, I came across a new breed to me, the Texel, smaller than the Kent but rounder than the Border Leicester, its main characteristic a very close wool. I rather hurried through the goat house, remembering the unnerving story of a parson friend who, when idly gazing at these animals, was suddenly asked to hold three on leading reins "just for a few minutes"; before their owner returned, he found himself being propelled with the other owners into the judging ring!

I definitely lingered at the main ring where I was fascinated by the Private Driving Class the elegance of each turn-out – horse, trap and driver (male and female), speaking of another age. Quite outstanding was a pair of small greys, drawing a superb four-

THE HARVEST FIELD
by C. Conway Plumbe

wheeled carriage, driven by mother and four year old son in sailor suit, with daughter in riding kit behind. It was such a lovely sight that it brought a lump to one's throat. The judges agreed and it won the championship. Finally, the Schools Stand, and conservation seemingly the main theme. Some very impressive displays, including the story of a Folkestone school's conversion of its disused swimming pool into an aquatic nature reserve.

To a Man of Kent, August conjures up visions of endless sunshine and Cricket Weeks. But towards the end comes St. Bartholomew's Day which reminds one of months to come. "If St. Bartholomew's be fine and clear, You may hope for a prosperous autumn that year."

Today has not, I fear, been truly "fine and clear" but cloudy and a little rain, so we may be in for a wet and windy autumn. However, the summer has been lovely and one of the resulting pleasures has been the sight of numerous butterflies, mainly common ones like peacocks, red admirals, tortoiseshells, gatekeepers, meadow browns and common blues, but sadly no commas in the fields round the rectory and Sandhurst Cross. Plenty of moths, too, like the square spot rustic and, the last few evenings, a veritable invasion through my study window of a tiny "stick" moth (real name unknown to me).

Visiting in Newenden today yielded two further pleasures – the sight of ten or more swallows on the wires at Lossenham (a slight rarity this year) and a good bird recovery story. John Cooper, hearing a bang on his window, discovered outside a stunned kingfisher. Warmth, patience and George Delemare's help brought partial recovery and limited movement but a reluctance to fly off over Hexden; it was not until four days later, after feeding and care at the Rye Reserve, that it finally chose to return to the wild near Peasmarsh. What a privilege, too, to look at a kingfisher for more than a few seconds.

Writing only two days before the end of August, I find that my rain-gauge has recorded a mere 2mm in the month. Some pasture is beginning to show it and the mallards and Aylesburys were actually standing in the muddy water of the pond on Hawkhurst Moor.

SEPTEMBER

MOST English counties, thank goodness, still retain a few typical characteristics. At the wheel of the car, on a brief holiday, I turned a corner and saw a pheasant, motionless on a park wall, silhouetted against the afternoon sky. That pheasant was soon succeeded by other pheasants investigating the stubble and close by, a round, pebble church tower. I knew then I was in Norfolk.

A while later, the Cley marshes came into view and immediately I almost ran into a small group of people in barbours and woolly hats, binoculars in action, all intently staring up into a copse of mature beech trees. I had arrived on that stretch of coast that draws bird-watchers like a magnet. My own natural interest in people and things of the countryside paled beside the keenness, indeed the fanaticism of those 'twitchers' I saw last week.

The next day furtive enquiries revealed that the current excitement was the presence of a yellow-browed warbler, possibly in that very beech copse. What a remote chance – to spot that tiny bird, hardly bigger than a goldcrest, in those large leafy trees. A thousand to one, I suppose. Not for me. Oliver and I were prepared to face the strong north-east wind and rain and to walk the marshes twice daily, but no more. We sensed the romantic wildness of those marshes. We walked among great stretches of sea lavender, sea campion and thrift, their flowers almost finished. Sometimes we watched oystercatchers and redshank probing the mud-flats, the redshank often suspicious and 'bobbing'. One day when we had seen only herons and gulls, there suddenly came, close overhead, a flock of 20 Brent geese, following the coastline to Blakeney Point where hundreds spend the winter every year. One of the earliest gifts to the National Trust, the Point is the summer home for over eleven species of seabird, particularly the common and sandwich tern and, offshore, observers in small open ferry boats often see numbers of seals, summer and winter.

It is a different world from the Weald. It is a step nearer Nature in its harshness and rawness. In winter there must be the feeling of daily battle with the elements and yet closeness to the wild life. The names of streets and houses emphasise this, such as Pintail Avenue and Rocket House.

In Cley Post Office, beside a Jack Russell which bites anyone touching it, there is a large poster, headed "In case of flood, the siren will sound . . ." Memories of 1953, when flood waters overwhelmed families in their homes and some were only just rescued from tables floating on sea water only a few feet below the ceiling.

WIGEON MOVING OUT TO SEA
by Roland Green MBOU, FRSA

QUITE heavy rain fell last night, waking me, but much to the relief of all sorts of people, particularly perhaps of golf and cricket secretaries, who are faced with a ban on watering. All may be well now, as village cricket has only two to three weeks of the season left and Kent has one more home match at Canterbury. The famous Week at the end of July was, believe it or not, interrupted once by rain for 20 minutes; otherwise glorious sunshine.

The rain also reminded me what it was like to live in a Victorian terraced house, with all-night traffic below my window. Next door to daughter Penny's house was one that had been empty for over a year. Its tiny garden, measuring 15 yards by 5, was an intriguing sight. It was a close mass of growth and colour, mostly 5 feet high, a delightful contrast to the surrounding bricks and mortar. A careful study revealed golden rod, purple loosestrife, broad-leaved willow herb, the tall yellow tansy daisy, welted thistle, lots of everlasting pea growing up old trellis work, interspersed here and there with the bell-shaped flowers of hedge bindweed. Not much other weed, but a sycamore sapling was a head higher than the rest. There were usually some large white butterflies and a couple of red admirals – a mini nature reserve.

FARMERS would claim that life is not easy these days. They must try to be economically self-sufficient and yet they must not produce too much food. There is also the 1981 Wildlife and Countryside Act and some farmers and landowners have Sites of Special Scientific Interest, which they are required to protect. Nevertheless many are trying their best in a small way to be environmentally sensitive, as for example planting up spare corners of land with oak, beech and other broad-leaved species.

Strong winds and squally rain have dominated the countryside and our lives for the past week. Specially has it dominated the thoughts of farmers about to start hop-picking. The result has been some hop gardens are 'down', after the stormy weather. My farmer friend, Jeremy, faced with two gardens 'down' in Sandhurst, has sent an SOS to his pickers and started a week earlier than planned. Another farmer friend with two gardens partially 'down' has already started picking. This picture may well be repeated across the Weald. One should spare a thought for all hop-growers these next three weeks, faced with pickers who are keen but human, machinery which looks a little Heath Robinson but these days is vital, and weather which is unpredictable. Behind it all there is a good crop to be harvested.

FOR two week-ends, clerical duties have taken me to St. Mary's, Goudhurst, its ragstone tower dominant, with grand views all round the compass. Richard Church, the Kent author and one of the local Home Guard, records it as their most important observation post. "What memorable sights we saw from there in the Battle of Britain", he writes. He would have been interested in the small network of scaffolding visible on the very top, last week-end. The weather-vane had been removed for repair and refurbishing. What is not going to be repaired are two bullet holes in the brass-work. Were they the result of a Messerschmitt firing its machine-guns at the vigilant Home Guard or a Hurricane on a roof-top chase of a German fighter? If the former, did the Home Guard fire back or immediately assume a horizontal position?!

MOST people are woken by alarm clocks. In my case it is often a mallard. This morning the duck flew in at 5.30 a.m., loudly demanding breakfast. Bleary eyed and bare foot, I offered her the usual corn and bread. Ten minutes later she took off and flew low over the grazing sheep into the early morning mist. Hardly had I crawled back into bed, than another duck arrived; she is altogether quieter and more nervous but also enjoys her food. They are two of quite a number who have been regularly flying into our small lawn over these summer months. In April and early May there were two pairs, one drake obviously older and a little

arthritic. Incubation began in their chosen territory and then the ducks demanded urgent attention, the drakes usually coming later and with more leisure. With the young growing up, we saw none for a while and now at least three ducks have resumed their early morning visits. The drakes have long since wandered off and we may not see them till winter or the new mating season. All this one of the many pleasures of life in the country and also a glimpse of the normal mating and breeding cycle.

TODAY I shared in the funeral of a friend in that grand 14th century church of St. George's, Ivychurch. As I crossed the canal bridge at Appledore, I found two large families of mute swans (about 15 in all) circling the canal rather aimlesly and foraging under water for vegetation, nature's way of keeping weed under some sort of control, for which the National Trust who own that stretch of water must be thankful. Continuing along the Rhee Wall road, I saw one or two of the usual herons standing watchful in the dykes, and on both sides of the road fair numbers of lapwings, on both grass and arable, on the look-out for wireworms and leatherjackets, disturbed by recent harrowing.

So to the funeral at St. George's, with the clock stopped at half past six and some of the deceased's

MALLARDS SIESTA
by Winifred Austen RI, RE, FZS

family already gathering outside. My friend was a farmer's widow, a real native of Romney Marsh, who had lived till recently beneath the shadow of the church tower, most fortunately floodlit free each evening by the lights of the Bell Inn. She was, I venture to say, the old-fashioned farmer's wife, warm, motherly, busy and caring for family and neighbours in need; the sort of wife who baked twice a week and regularly produced good beef puddings, jam roly-polys and sloe wine when they were in season and there was a little spare time. Behind all she did was a simple but definite faith in God the Creator and an instinctive understanding that such a faith embraced worship in the parish church. A lovely person to have around – warm, smiling, hospitable, so from all there was much thanksgiving.

At the end, clergy and mourners escorted the coffin to the hearse, with some care, along the old, uneven red brick path on which weeds contended with confetti from a recent wedding. True rural conditions and characteristics, not the dull ordinariness of smooth suburban asphalt. Over on the northern churchyard boundary, the tall limes and turkey oaks were beginning to change colour and the rookery in the Old Rectory garden was alive and fairly noisy, but sadly the gate connecting churchyard and rectory was broken, tied up, unused and almost lost to view by foliage. Had the occupants of that rather lovely Georgian house (once my own home) forgotten about God?

THE weather seems to be breaking up and the nights are cooler. Autumnal signs include some leaf-fall from the churchyard limes, slght change in colour of the horse-chestnuts, a considerable drop of beech-mast and acorns and the green of the hedgerow and verge becoming faded and dust-covered. A twenty yard stretch of willow-lined dyke on the Levels exemplified the changing scene, a lovely medley of berries against the green foliage – orange-red hips, claret-coloured haws, black and red blackberries and jet black elderberries, the whole vaguely gathered together by innumerable stems of bindweed and its white flowers; an artistic offering by Nature.

OCTOBER

THIS first week-end in October usually sees the last cricket match of the season and the Weald of Kent Ploughing Match. Fortunately the sun shone brightly for Newenden's cricketers for their final game against Outwood, Surrey. The spirit was in the best village cricket tradition, keen but friendly, and the game was enhanced by two towering 6's over the limes into the main road by Guy, Newenden's captain, and some excellent refreshments with buffet by the chairman in the nearby White Hart. Edmund Blunden, the Kent poet, would have approved. He might have wished for more deckchairs and coloured blazers but the atmosphere was in tune with his own attitude, summarized in "Cricket Country" – "In our village and county, the game was so native, so constant, so beloved without fuss that it came to me as the air I breathed and the morning and evening".

Arriving a little late at the Ploughing Match at Linton, I was soon involved. John Bourne & Co. offered instant hospitality in the shape of beef-burgers and red wine and dynamic Oliver demanded immediate transfer to the Terrier Show round the corner. Not surprisingly, the atmosphere was electric. About sixty JRs were giving tongue incessantly, simultaneously, competing success-fully with the staccato noise of clay pigeon shooting 200 yards away. Nevertheless, at the expense of some spilled wine balanced by discipline, we stood firm until the highlight of the afternoon – the terrier racing. In the meantime we circulated among the stalls, almost all closely related to farming and the countryside, and offering advice and quotations on such things as trenching and impact moling, as well as waxed cotton jackets to keep you dry from the imminent rain. Among the many farming friends encountered, it was good to find a Cabinet Minister sharing the interests of his constituents.

To the uninitiated, I can only repeat that the highlight, perhaps the climax, of the afternoon is the terrier racing. Character, vitality and variety are all present. Excitement is intense, the noise considerable and a large crowd assembles behind the flimsy barriers to see the fun. Heats are run at five minute intervals for half an hour or more. Anything may happen, and does. But the *piéce de resistance* came in the two finals – large Jack Russells and smaller ones. In the first, a labrador decided to cross the track as the terriers emerged from their starting boxes, causing several to swerve sharply and one, Toggle, champion though he was, to give up completely. In the second, the start was delayed because the wheel operating "that thing" had broken down. So the stalwart organisers commandeered an athletic small boy to be

AUTUMN PLOUGHING
by Martin Hardie RWS, RSW, RE

the 'hare' with the 'brush' attached to his rear. To the crowds' delight, the leading terrier caught the 'hare' and carried the 'brush' away to his owner's car.

IT WAS 12.30pm and the Marden Fruit Show luncheon was about to begin. Over 200 people, representing fruit growing and marketing, were seated in the big marquee, with the Cranbrook School Light Orchestra offering us pleasant background music. An Elizabethan grace from the Vicar of Marden launched us into a thoroughly good lunch, washed down inevitably by either cider or apple juice. Professor Colin Spedding, Chairman of the Apple and Pear Research Council, proved himself an admirable guest speaker, mixing information and wit in a remarkable way. He seemed to have an endless store of (so-called) Chinese proverbs as well as the ability to produce 'off the cuff' comments at will – the sudden violent flapping of the marquee during his speech brought "You see the effect of hot air!". And when his eye caught the question blazoned on the marquee "Is there a Bramley in your family?", he advised a further question "Have you a Cox in the car?". Good, skilful speaking. After further speeches came the presentation of the numerous cups and trophies, headed by an amazing list of awards all won by the same farm and received by Mrs. A. M. Bardsley.

Later, of course, we all did several circuits of the Show itself and probably spent more time talking to friends than examining the superb apples and pears, all beautifully packed and exhibited. One entry, though, exhibited the heaviest apple, 2lb. 3oz, again won by J. Scott. What a dumpling it would make! A meal almost for a family.

Fruit Show though it may be, it was being held in the Weald of Kent and there just had to be a small corner for hops, and a photocopy of a very old poster intrigued me. It was headed "Hop Saturday" and wording and lay-out went as follows:

Monster Hop Demonstration
(non-political)
to endeavour to save the English hop gardens
MASS MEETING IN TRAFALGAR SQUARE
on May 16th 1908 at 4pm
Speakers include: a Brewer, an Allied Trader, Father Wilson (East London), an East Kent working man, a London hop-picker, a Worcester working man, Rev. Mr Mart(South London).

Sadly, times repeat themselves

AUTUMN temporarily became winter last Thursday, 17th – north-west wind and an overcast sky, so my duffle coat came out for the first time and we lit a fire. So things have remained for the last three days, but, being dry, work has continued apace on the farms. On nearby Hole Park Farm, linseed has been harvested, apple-picking completed and the hops, hitherto retained, are now able to go to the central hop store at Paddock Wood which was badly damaged by fire a few weeks ago.

The new harvest is already showing its head. Thanks to the spell of warm sunny weather and some rain earlier in the month, winter wheat has emerged, ten days after drilling. On another field on the Rother Levels the efficient power harrow has broken up the furrows preparatory to more drilling. On the old drovers' road alongside, dragon-flies are still zooming around, in spite of the north-west winds; mid-afternoon, with a slight rise in temperature and some sun, they are out and about, often with a few small whites.

UMBRELLA stands are an endlessly fascinating study. They inevitably reveal the personalities and interests of the family or householder, providing the observant visitor is left alone in the hall for five minutes. My own umbrella stand, banished, I hope temporarily, to the garage for lack of room in the hall, contains six hockey sticks, three cricket bats, three golf clubs, two walking sticks, one shooting-stick and no umbrellas. Conclusions are not difficult.

The umbrella stand of friends living in Wiltshire differed only a little, in that it lacked the cricket bats (Wiltshire is, of course, in the Minor County Championship!) but it did have three umbrellas, one of them a golf one, dwarfing everything else. That of another friend on the Kent coast, observed a few weeks ago, was flamboyantly different. Its base was mounted onto rhinoceros feet and it was completely dominated by hats (which normally reveal current emotion as well as permanent personality). These hats crowning the sticks and umbrellas, were of the informal, floppy, woollen type, including one from Swaledale, another from Ireland, yet another from Portugal (a rather stiff panama) and, just visible, great gran's umbrella. Dare anyone open it up?

Having said all this, is an umbrella really part of the true countryman's equipment? Is it not rather a case of wellies, waterproofs and a good stout hat or cap? Nevertheless, most people, country or town, are wise to keep one in the car. You never know if the weather is going to turn a somersault.

A KENTISH MILL
by J. C. T. Willis

NOVEMBER

LAST Sunday I became once more a real country parson. I spent the day on the North Downs, leading worship in three tiny parish churches in a truly rural situation. No main road within miles, no bus services, just farms, woods, lots of rabbits scampering into the verges and pheasants calmly strolling around like lords and ladies. Indeed there was a whiff of the feudal present in the churches and it was undoubtedly stabilising and reassuring to those faithful country folk and to me.

At my 8 o'clock Communion the squire, who is churchwarden and also a national figure, was present with his wife. At my later Parish Communion, memorials to the Tylden family at Milstead Manor competed silently with the longevity and sheer strength of the Norman pillar and arch in the chancel. At Evensong the current squire was bellringer, organist, choir and, later, host at his historical house, supported by a vocal peacock. Somehow it works. Whatever the modernists and cynics may say, the congregations were larger, in proportion to the total population, than those in any Wealden town church.

THE cherry tree near the house seems to glow Its. 'warmth' in the early morning sun is reflected on the interior walls. I often declare that the finest natural sight in Kent is a cherry orchard in full blossom, but I should add that those same trees in their autumn coat of gold and pink also deserve a pause in quiet admiration.

My cherry tree is, of course, characteristic of much lovely autumn colouring all around us in the Weald. The frosts and the rain of October have combined to bring about this annual spectacle this first week of November. Green Lane, Rolvenden, leading through Backtilt Wood to Benenden Hospital is typical; beech trees predominate, with rabbits, pheasants, squirrels and the occasional badger all very much present and lending movement to the lovely, leafy scene.

Why do so many rush to sweep up autumn leaves? Sometimes safety requires it, perhaps on a brick path, and sometimes the devotion of a gardener to his lawn drives him and his rake into action. But often they can be left to the whims of Nature and the elements to rearrange, perhaps around herbaceous plants (thus protecting against severe frost) or piled up in ever changing shapes against fences and walls. Also large herbaceous plants, supplemented by leaves, are often home for the winter to hibernating hedgehogs, whom we all love to have around our gardens. So, I like to go easy with the spring rake and garden broom and let Nature relieve me of some of that work.

LARDERS are exciting places for small children. They are also exciting places for mice. We suspected that we had them in our larder but we were not prepared for what we found the other day. My wife was engaged in a real turn-out and this included a sack full of empty jam jars. One jar, lying on its side, was not empty but full, full of Winalot (from a nearby bag) and pieces of plastic sack. One mouse – one suspects a field mouse – more prudent and foreseeing than most, must have decided to forgo the feast and prepare for the winter. I cannot see an ordinary house mouse resisting the desire to eat anything eatable. So there it was – a winter store, roughly covered up by pieces of black plastic.

LAST week I visited the smallest parish church in England. The only way to get there was to walk, two and a half miles of loose stone and slate track, climbing and descending, entirely wooded, sloping on one side down to the shore. Finally, we saw it – Culbone Church, nestling in a tiny valley clearing, with its minute churchyard, two houses and lovely clear stream. Inside, 15th century screen and seating, enough perhaps for twenty; candles the only means of light, on chandelier and on harmonium.

Peaceful and utterly remote, and yet, to our surprise, they had one service a Sunday and occasional baptisms, weddings and funerals, as recent tombstones showed (and how right that they should be of slate). But what about the coffin? It must be a case of landrover along our track or boat and tractor and trailer from the shore. Even the bishop walks, so he told me the next day in Wells. Gathering strength we made rather better progress on the return journey to the car for a very late lunch. Suitably strengthened we began our climb up to the main road, two miles of really narrow lane, bordered on both sides by the typical Devon/Somerset bank-cum-hedge. It only needed the plaintive mewing of the buzzard circling overhead to complete the satisfying picture.

VIEWING the marsh yesterday from Sandhurst churchyard I realised I could only just distinguish the Rother. There was just a semblance of river bank showing in the wide expanse of floods. What rain! I have not read any official figures but I was told of one Sussex farmer who had measured 18 inches in the nine weeks beginning the 1st September. Such was the flooding at Etchingham, too, that one expected any day the tired commuters to find their cars parked in a foot of water.

How are the pheasants and partridge faring, I wonder? Twice this week, on separate days, a noticeably wet and bedraggled cock pheasant has lifted itself across the lane. They must long for the shelter and dryness of something like a really thick beech hedge, with its leaves still holding or a closely

AUTUMN
by E. W. Haslehust RI

packed copse. Wild stormy weather almost certainly caused an unusual sighting for Mr. and Mrs. Rummery. Twice in one evening, a month ago, they disturbed a black redstart sheltering inside their porch.

Another unusual report comes from David Cole, just returned from a week on board Shell's derrick ship building a new oil rig. Present on board and audible at night is a tawny owl, living somewhere up aloft in the giant crane – 150 miles from land and the ship only putting into port every three months! What does it feed on – unless rats and mice come up on deck or small birds alight from time to time?

FOR eight consecutive days at the end of November there was an extraordinary stillness in the countryside. One could hear a field mouse foraging among the beech leaves, a dog barking two miles, away and the Kent and East Sussex Railway engine drawing out of Wittersham Road station when fishing near Maytham Wharf. The time could be 12 noon, not midnight. A bonfire could always be lit within a yard or two of the dividing fence and one's neighbour's washing, without the fear of angry words or court action. Such was the calm, one felt at peace. Today, the church weather vane points north-east, there is a cold breeze and Mr. Ron Lobeck hints at the possibility of a white Christmas. The weather is changing.

This evening "Country Ways" of TVS carried me in mind's eye to Guernsey, the home of those lovely cows and of glasshouses filled with tomatoes. We met a farmer, a fisherman, a silversmith, a woodworker and a goatkeeper. "No foxes or badgers", the farmer said, "so no need to shut up the chickens". Yet his constant companion was a Jack Russell who chivvied the cows, checked on the pigs and was co-driver of the pony-trap when on a training run for the young horse. A typical Jack Russell, some will think.

To me, as I watched, the point that emerged, above all others, was the contentment of those interviewed. Craftsmanship, set in the countryside, brought peace of mind. It also involved, in most cases, the family. A son sat, cross-legged, making lobster pots, another decorated wooden figures; a wife struggled with the goats. Their faces were lined and weather-beaten but relaxed. They seemed happy.

DECEMBER

TODAY as usual, my robin was waiting for me. He seems to have adopted me in the same way as others adopt householders at their backdoors or kitchen windows. As I park my car at the old mounting block at the churchyard, there he is on the sheep-gate or the fence. Admittedly he usually expects and gets a few titbits but, even after two months, he still moves into the overhanging lime branch as a safety precaution whilst I scatter his breakfast. Like all robins he is fiercely territorial and is rarely more than 20 yards from that spot. Only in the coldest weather, when food is paramount, will robins allow other robins to invade their territory.

About ten days ago, on a very frosty morning, a blackbird was allowed to share his meal and both were being watched by a kestrel perched on a nearby tombstone. I cannot help but wonder whether this robin was one of a pair which nested last summer deep into the mass of suckers growing out of the base of the great old lime close by; superbly hidden and safe from most predators.

"A PARTRIDGE in a pear-tree . . ." so runs the Christmas song; but Roderick, my friend, has another version. A few days back, walking through his farmyard, he was astonished to see fifteen or so partridges lined up at eave level on his oast. "They seemed to be having a good argument, too" he said. As they were the French, red-legged variety, this high perch, while unusual, is a little less surprising than with our native grey partridge. Red-legged "cousin" often perches to make its distinctive, loud, challenging call. This it would not find very easy on Romney Marsh where I understand from Peter Playford a fair number were released this autumn not far from the Appledore-Rye stretch of the canal.

Whether French or English variety, they seem to have a harder fight for survival these days than most game birds. Contending, when young, with foxes and weasels, sometimes food shortage and pesticides, or simply bad weather in the breeding season, and later with guns and precious little cover, they deserve our admiration and interest. Turning to winter visitors – I have the impression of fewer fieldfares than usual, perhaps because of a shortage of rotting apples; redwings were about in fair numbers down Crouch Lane yesterday, roaming the fields with song thrushes and lapwings.

MY commitments also took me down last week to Snave church in Romney Marsh, a church well-known for its broad avenue of daffodils *en masse*. Just three houses keep it company and, two hundred

UPLANDS OF KENT
by Martin Hardie RWS, RSW, RE

yards away, one of the few remaining looker's huts, where the 'looker' or shepherd spent many long hours during lambing time. Little shelter, too, for wild life. "Not many foxes, but a fair number of badgers," according to my farmer-churchwarden friend, who thought the numerous mink had decimated the mallard and moorhen. Nearby is Hangman's Field where miscreants were buried after being hanged in Maidstone or at the local gallows, and in the churchyard stands a visible link with those days, two simple headstones with names, that were rescued from the dyke a few years ago.

Inside the church there are the barest simplest furnishings, in keeping with a redundant church, but still full of interest and history and proudly displaying its Royal Coat of Arms. The lighting is only by candle, but nothing is more beautiful and meaningful than a lighted candle, whether in a lonely Marsh church or Bath Abbey.

NINE days to Christmas and I am at once conscious of a contrast. Whether shopping in Tenterden High Street or driving along the A21, there is the sense of bustle and haste. Yet on the Rother Levels or in the fields behind my house, all is normal. Nature is quite unaffected and how greatly stabilising this is. Our pair of mallard flew in as usual for their feed; the dykes frozen for a week, reacted to higher temperatures, not Christmas fever; and the front page photo of *The Times* today showed swans and geese at Slimbridge, at rest or gently cruising. Nature is always a soothing antidote, and what clear bright days and lovely red sunsets we have been enjoying, too!

So, Christmas in the country brings us all down to earth. The stock still have to be fed, the dogs walked and the chickens shut up, for fear of the fox. Often, too, in the Weald there is the log fire in the large inglenook fireplace, able to seat one or two either side. The rush of the M25 or London's Oxford Street is forgotten. With a little quiet and thought we may be able to recollect what it is really all about.

Householders increasingly put up fine, illuminated Christmas trees in their front gardens, reminding us of the festive season but not proclaiming the kernel of the Festival. Benenden and Staplehurst churches do rather better; each has a large illuminated star on their tower. Inside, most churches declare the Christmas message through music, drama and colourful ceremony. Staplehurst's Christingle Service was typical. Step by step, a few brief simple words (interspersed with singing) explained the christingle, symbolizing God's saving act for His world, proclaimed that evening by the lighting of 180 candles. The children loved it. In many faces there was delight, wonder and awe. An example for us all as we celebrate the most wonderful birth of all time.

IT IS a week before Christmas and I sleepily look

out of the bedroom window about 7 a.m. The eastern sky is light enough to etch the trees above the rectory pond and also movement and outline on the lawns below. A fox, sitting on his haunches, scratching vigorously! Then he investigates the roots of the great Scots pine, still recumbent, the last survivor from our casualties of the Great Storm, hoping for mice or beetles still active in the early morning twilight. But he was disappointed and eventually lolloped along the herbaceous borders, past the vegetable garden and into the neighbouring orchard.

Meanwhile I descend and walk Oliver round the garden. He picks up the fox's scent at once but, after frenzied to-ing and fro-ing, has to be content with a few sharp chases of numerous blackbirds enjoying the early worm. His special hate is, I suppose, our grey squirrels. They are not yet around, preferring full daylight for feeding on the plentiful acorns and beechmast available and also around or on our bird table. These are now needed, especially when there is a sustained period of freezing temperatures and hard ground surfaces.

An architect friend, recently inspecting a house on the edge of Romney Marsh, came across a plastic nut container hanging on the house wall, with a field mouse at the bottom, too fat after its feast to climb up. For him slimming was indeed a matter of life or death.

St. Thomas' Day is imminent. Country lore urges one to look at the weather vane that day; the wind will remain in that quarter for three months! It is the traditional day also for "begging by poor women" and, therefore, the annual payments by some charities, just in time for recipients to enjoy a better Christmas.

But what can be more uplifting and moving than Midnight Communion in the quietness of a medieval country church? Churchgoers and 'fringers' unite in their desire to celebrate the most important birth in the history of the world. Candles, words and music combine to shape this special offering of praise by the creature to the Creator. "In the beginning was the Word . . . and the Word was made flesh and dwelt among us."

THE EDGE OF THE WOOD
by Roland Green MBOU, FRSA

Martin Hardie